The Pea That Was Me
...and Me
...and Me!

(How All Kinds of Babies Are Made)

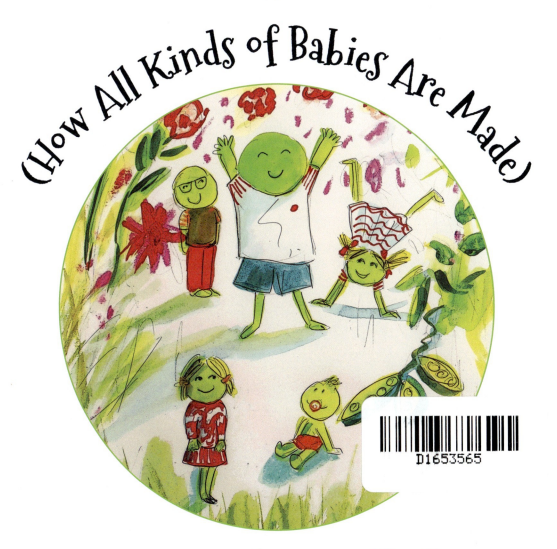

Kim Kluger-Bell

Illustrated by Ros Webb

For All the Miracle Children of the World,
Their Courageous Parents,
and Their Gracious Donors and Surrogates

Copyright © 2018 Kimberly Kluger-Bell

All rights reserved.

ISBN-13 978-1985582293

ISBN 1985582295

My mom came home today with some really BIG NEWS!

And whoever it was, they were already growing in her tummy!

Mom said wishes were part of it but ...

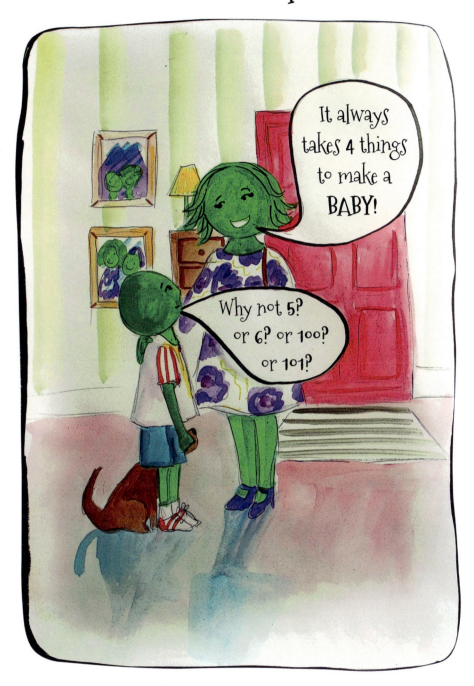

(I didn't know WHAT she was talking about.)

My mom just smiled.

(Also called her uterus!)

(It was COOL.)

(With Daddy's sperm and Mommy's eggs and tummy!)

I.V.F.

Mom said a DOCTOR HELPED my
Aunt Shirley & Uncle Turley have
my (crazy) COUSINS LARRY & SHERRY.

They wished for a baby but couldn't make a pea,
so they went to a DOCTOR who put

Shirley's EGGS with Turley's SPERM and made
2 pea embryos that grew into Sherry & Larry.

SPERM DONATION

AND my (new) best friend Jason's MOM & DAD needed help from a VERY NICE MAN ...

JASON (He's a great soccer player!)

who gave them an AMAZING GIFT to make JASON.

Their sperm DONOR

(They haven't met him, but someday they might.)

SINGLE MOM SPERM DONATION

My kindergarten teacher, MS. TERRI, had her little girl this way too.

(They look just alike!)

She also had the help of a SPERM DONOR.

(BUT NOT the same one!)

2 MOMS SPERM DONATION

I also found out my neighbor AMBER'S TWO MOMS had the help of a SPERM DONOR

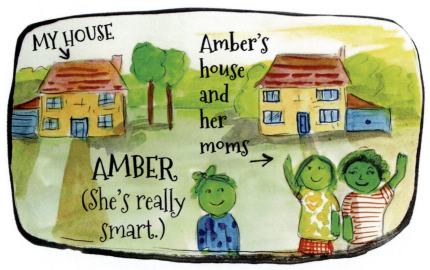

who gave them the sperm they needed to make AMBER.

(Their DONOR was a good friend of theirs.)

SINGLE MOM EGG + SPERM DONATION

My friend TINA'S Aunt (the one who just had a baby) had LOTS of help.

She had the help of a DOCTOR, an EGG DONOR, and a SPERM DONOR.

EMBRYO DONATION

My GUITAR TEACHER and her husband had a lot of help too, to have their son JACK.

A DOCTOR

A nice woman & man who had an embryo

(Sometimes single moms, 2 moms, or 2 dads need this kind of help.)

GESTATIONAL CARRIER

And my **soccer coach & his husband** are getting the help of a GESTATIONAL CARRIER to have their baby.

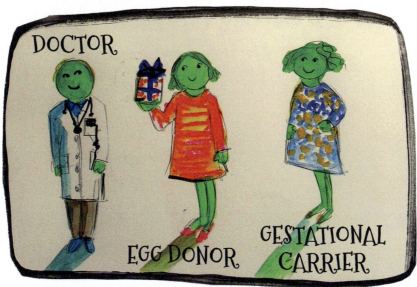

They ALSO had the help of a doctor and an EGG DONOR!

EGG DONATION

All of this was **AMAZING**, but I still wanted to know how **OUR** new baby was going to come to be.

Nope! It was with the help of an **EGG DONOR** (and a doctor).

So the way I came to be, and the way our NEW BABY will come to be is DIFFERENT...

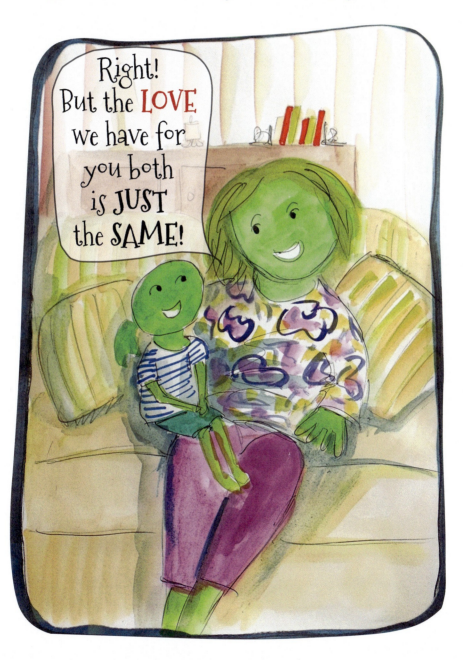

And that's TRUE for ALL KIDS:

IVF KIDS — Like my cousins LARRY & SHERRY

SPERM DONOR KIDS — Like my buddy JASON

Single MOM SPERM DONOR KIDS — Like my kindergarten teacher's LITTLE GIRL

2 MOMS SPERM DONOR KIDS — Like my neighbor AMBER

Single MOM EGG + SPERM DONOR KIDS

EMBRYO DONOR KIDS

KIDS carried by SURROGATES or GESTATIONAL CARRIERS

EGG DONOR KIDS

IT ALL STARTS with LOVE
in the hearts of your parents.

And NO MATTER HOW YOU came to be, PARENTS LOVE all their children NO MATTER WHAT!!

THE END

(But wait! One more thing...
Turn the page!)

My Family Came to Be Like This:

MY NAME: Peater Vinny

HOW I CAME TO BE: With Mom and Dad's love, but without any other special helpers.

MY NEW SISTER OR BROTHER: With the help of an egg donor and a doctor.

WHAT WE KNOW ABOUT OUR DONOR: She is a very nice person who wanted to help a family like us have another baby.

OUR DOCTOR'S NAME: I don't know I have to ask my mom and dad.

OUR CLINIC'S NAME: Not sure about that either …

What About Your Family?

YOUR NAME: _____

DID YOU HAVE ANY SPECIAL HELPERS? _____

_____

IF YES, WAS IT AN EGG DONOR, A SPERM DONOR, BOTH, AN EMBRYO DONOR OR A GESTATIONAL CARRIER (SURROGATE)?

_____

_____

WHAT DO YOU KNOW ABOUT THESE HELPERS? _____

_____

WHAT WAS YOUR DOCTOR'S NAME? _____

AND THE CLINIC'S NAME? _____

More About Your Family...

YOUR SISTER OR BROTHER'S NAME: _____

DID SHE OR HE HAVE ANY SPECIAL HELP: _____
_____

IF YES, WAS IT AN EGG DONOR, A SPERM DONOR, BOTH, AN EMBRYO DONOR OR A GESTATIONAL CARRIER (SURROGATE)?
_____
_____

WHAT DO YOU KNOW ABOUT THESE HELPERS? _____
_____

WHAT WAS YOUR DOCTOR'S NAME? _____

AND THE CLINIC? _____

Your Family, continued . . .

YOUR OTHER SISTER OR BROTHER'S NAME: _____

DID SHE OR HE HAVE ANY SPECIAL HELP: _____
_____

IF YES, WAS IT AN EGG DONOR, A SPERM DONOR, BOTH, AN EMBRYO DONOR OR A GESTATIONAL CARRIER (SURROGATE)?
_____
_____

WHAT DO YOU KNOW ABOUT THESE HELPERS? _____
_____

WHAT WAS YOUR DOCTOR'S NAME? _____

AND THE CLINIC? _____

Here's a place to draw a picture of your family or paste a photograph: